THE HOMES OF FOOTBALL

Where the Heart is

The Photographs of Stuart Roy Clarke

The Bluecoat Press

“Our game, in the country where I was raised, is not about ‘Ultras’ or megaphones, flares, fences and moats. It’s a heart-thumping love-letter to ourselves. You show me anything in British life that is more silly, more important, more engaging than this football fayre.”

Stuart Roy Clarke

Introduction

Colin Wilkinson, Bluecoat Press

Like so many other football supporters, my first football match is indelibly lodged in my brain. I was a late starter at thirteen and chose a cracker of a match for my first experience: Sheffield Wednesday versus Birmingham City. The Owls won 5–0 with a hat-trick from David ‘Bronco’ Layne, whose promising career was cut short two seasons later when he was imprisoned for his part in a betting scandal. I was hooked, not just on the football which passed by in a blur, but on the sight and sound of a sea of men in flat caps (it was mainly men in those days), smoking their Woodies or Parkies on Hillsborough’s all-standing Kop. The following week, I watched Sheffield United demolish Tottenham Hotspur, the first double-winners of the modern game. Greaves, Blanchflower and Mackay facing the cutting edge of Steel City. The emphatic 3–1 victory for the Blades and the crowd breaking into that old Yorkshire anthem *On Ilkla Moor baht ’at* almost got me but I was not one of those fickle supporters who switched allegiance at the drop of an ’at. Blue was my colour – at least until I moved to Liverpool a decade later and realised that watching a team that actually won things had distinct advantages (I clung on until 1978, when Wednesday’s ignominious 1-0 defeat in the FA Cup to non-league Wigan Athletic convinced me that Saturday afternoons could be better spent).

In over fifty years, I have watched hundreds of games, drawn as much by the ritual of live football as the match itself. I have seen it all – the violence and tragedy as well as the joy and good humour. Swaying on the Anfield Kop with supporters breaking into impromptu song was unforgettable, as was taking my son to his first match, ironically against Sheffield Wednesday at Anfield, when Liverpool inexplicably lost 2-0. My son had no time for such setbacks having spent the whole match looking in wonder at the crowd rather than the game.

This is what the game is about. The headlines may be dominated by the top teams in the Premiership and the antics of a select few players but the real story is the passion so many of us have for the game. In Stuart Roy Clarke, we have someone who really understands what it means to its millions of supporters. His travels have taken him from the meanest of grounds to the most palatial and, whether photographing a pair of goalposts in an overgrown field to a capacity Old Trafford, he has captured a sense of place, and that place is England.

For twenty-five years, Clarke has set out on a unique mission to celebrate the game so dear to him. *The Homes of Football* is not just another football book, it is an outstanding document of a nation's passion. It will appeal to people who might not normally be interested in the game. As you turn its pages, it speaks the language of English football (albeit with a cacophony of accents to choose from). He is proud of what his country has offered in the name of football in the 150 years since it invented 'The Rules'. His photography, though inspired by all of football's history, covers the years since the Hillsborough disaster in 1989, his starting point.

The images are beautifully taken and presented and yet often of mundane moments and places. Clarke's pictures at first impression look shiny and new and it's hard to believe they were taken as long ago as 1989, until one looks at the detail and the content. Much of what is shown has now gone. Many of his pictures are of things (a ticket office, a licensed bar, a piece of graffiti) that you and I would have seen for ourselves at the time but, as is the skill of an artist, Clarke has transformed them into memorable images

.

This book is defined by Clarke in three parts covering twenty-five years: there is the early "inspired" work, then the "churning over the subject again and again", then a final chapter of new work not published before "clearly showing my heart is more in it then ever".

His photographs are preceded by his map of Britain: clubs and places Clarke has already visited. His ninety-two-year old uncle when imprisoned abroad during the Second World War would recreate a map of England through its football clubs, grounds and nicknames. Now, in an old peoples' home, he is doing it again. Clarke junior for his part, based in remote Cumbrian countryside for the entire span of *The Homes of Football*, counts clubs instead of sheep to get himself to sleep. Thankful that this is peacetime and he can devote as much time again as he already has to *The Homes of Football*.

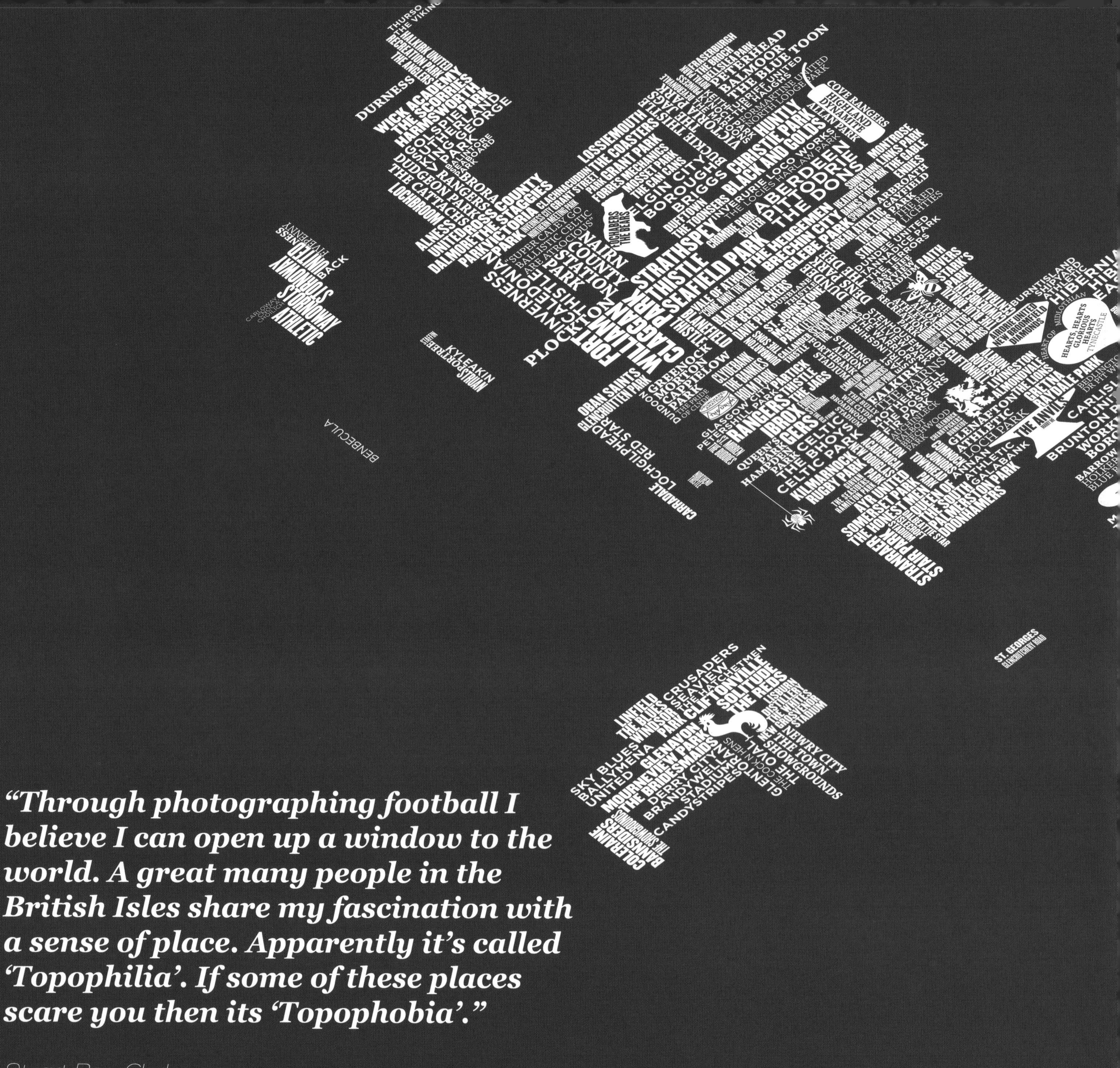

"Through photographing football I believe I can open up a window to the world. A great many people in the British Isles share my fascination with a sense of place. Apparently it's called 'Topophilia'. If some of these places scare you then its 'Topophobia'."

Stuart Roy Clarke

Stuart Roy Clarke's "Green and Pleasant Land"

Stuart Roy Clarke has been to most of these grounds, valuing the big and the small in equal measure through his work.

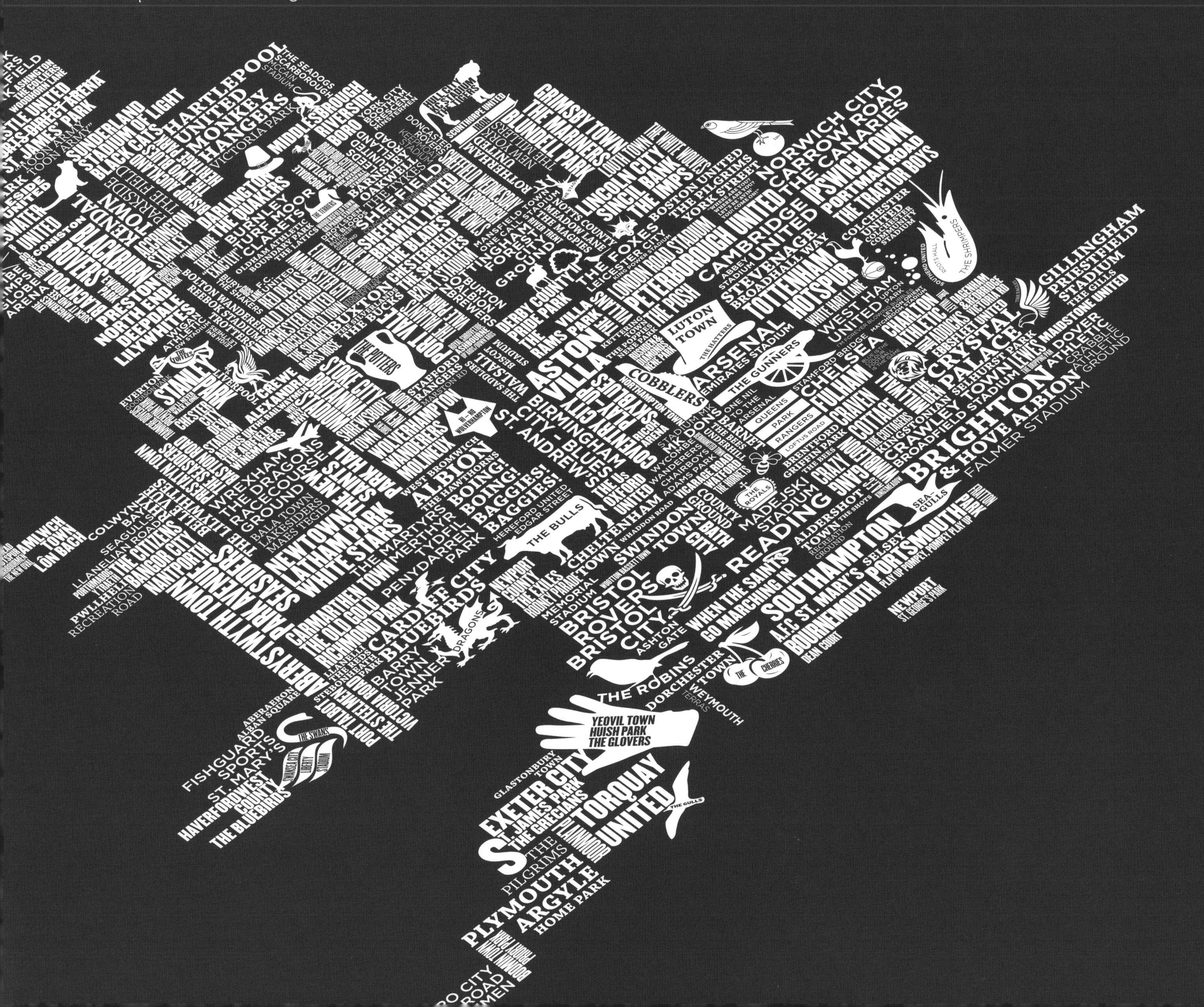

FOOTBALL GROUND
ME PRODUCE

"One Way Home" Stockport County, 1990

Foreword

by John Williams & Andrew Ward from "Football Nation"

Stuart Roy Clarke took his first football photograph at Vicarage Road, Watford, in the mid-1970s. That day, he played truant from Saturday lessons at his grammar-school, caught the train, walked to the Watford ground and snuck his Instamatic camera through the turnstile. He had all day Sunday to think up an excuse for missing school.

As a young boy, watching Watford alongside his father and brother, Clarke spent half his time studying the people. He was fascinated by the crowd. At home he drew pictures of stadiums and spectators. Out and about, he took photogaphs with classic cameras. When he began hitch-hiking, he found that the fate of football teams was a guaranteed starting point for conversation.

After the 1989 Hillsborough Disaster, Clarke realised that something of national importance was decaying or dying. During the early 1990s, professional clubs were undoubtedly in a sad financial state, but Clarke saw beauty in the squalor of the grounds he visited. He decided to capture some of football's former glories before they became like the ruins of Rome. He started work on a photographic collection called *The Homes of Football*.

After slipping through a crack in the gate and bypassing the ticket office at the new Wycombe Wanderers ground ('a bit like an industrial unit'), he took a famous picture of BBC commentator John Motson talking live to camera in a blizzard. At Blackburn, his shot of a man waving a crutch to celebrate a Manchester City goal (and the club's second successive promotion) portrayed football's healing powers. And "Sunset over Springfield Park", taken at Wigan Athletic's unfashionable ground, preserved a stereotypical sunset scene with blurred figures that seemed to represent ghostly generations of dreamy fans. The image was made all the more poignant by Wigan's later departure from Springfield Park (in 1999) and their propulsion towards the FA Premier League.

Realising that he was on to something, Clarke travelled around the homes of football, from one fascinating football place to another, capturing images of character and substance. He understood that fans found real meaning in the detail of football grounds: the first sight of a floodlight pylon or a grandstand roof; the fanzine-sellers on the approach to the stadium; a 'Players and Officials Only' sign; a coach with the visiting team's name on the side; a rickety tea-hut; the half-time scoreboard; a coracle outside Shrewsbury Town's Gay Meadow ground (to collect the ball when it went in the river); a Bradford City staircase painted yellow to symbolise safety; a rolled-up match-day programme in a clenched fist; a distant view of hospitality boxes; and even football graffiti. He discovered that each ground had something distinctive. He loved the slightly scary walk to Burnley's Turf Moor, with the occasional view of the Pennines, the sun low on the Towneley-side streets as queues formed in the chip shop. He was particularly pleased when he took his *Looking Up* picture of fans at Sunderland. It captured generations together, a thousand mouths ajar, heroic and wondrous people in red–and–white–striped shirts, somehow affirming football's post–Hillsborough meaning. Stuart Roy Clarke built up a rich body of photographic art that portrayed the English national spirit through England's national sport.

Geographers use the concept of *topophilia* – the love of place. Football fans, as much as anybody, have strong emotional ties to the material environment. Regular visitors to a football ground grow to appreciate the quirks of familiar surroundings. They accept defects and discomforts, rather like the stereotypical old man who sits in his favourite chair (despite its faulty springs) with pipe, slippers and newspaper at hand, perfectly content even though he knows that the house needs decorating and the roof leaks. By the early 1990s, the average English top-division stadium was the old man of Europe, eighty–eight years old, far older than the average stadium in Germany (forty–eight) and Italy (thirty–seven).

Like an old man's home, a football ground can represent a castle, a theatre, a fortress, a refuge, a shrine, a cathedral, a site for a political rally or a tourist resort. A stadium is literally *our home ground*. It is a sacred place where feelings can be shown and you can be yourself. It is a therapy centre. It is a place for intimacy.

"You are close to the public," Frenchman Eric Cantona said in the early 1990s, comparing English grounds with those in other European countries. "It is warmer. There is room for love."

Very different to topophilia is *topophobia* – the fear of a place. Some rival grounds scare fans. At times, during the hooliganism era, their home ground did too. Some grounds felt like prisons. Fences and walls were built, dangerous objects were confiscated, CCTV footage recorded your every move, and police supervision matched that of prison warders. But the rump of fans still thought of their stadium as home. It still gave them an uplifting feeling on arrival. They enjoyed the smells of the grilled food, the sounds of the crowd and the Tannoy system, and the visual pleasures of a green canvas dotted with colours.

Some fans have visited their football ground more times than they have visited a close relative (or even a workplace). They understand the impact of the weather on the pitch, the angle of the sun in different seasons, the wind direction, and they can guess the attendance by a mere glance at a few telling areas of the ground.

Stuart Roy Clarke intuitively understood this culture. Football grounds were Dickensian and dilapidated but they were also soaked in meaningful history. Southend United's Roots Hall had subsiding terraces built over a rubbish tip, three stands clad in asbestos and crush barriers that could be shaken loose, but it was still home, and some fans had been visiting it since it opened in 1955. Teams, managers, directors and players come and go, the kit changes from time to time, but a club's football ground remained a constant ... until the early 1990s, that is, when the homes of football began to change radically.

In his report on the Hillsborough Disaster, Lord Justice Taylor stipulated that all Football League grounds should be all-seated for safety reasons. In 1990, John Major reduced the pools' companies' spot-the-ball duty from 42½% to 40% (despite resistance from Treasury staff who thought that football was awash with money) with the proviso that the difference went to the Football Trust for grants to help upgrade the major stadiums. The Taylor proposal was soon limited to the top two English divisions (and the Scottish Premier League). By the end of August 1996, the Football Trust, having received £127m via the betting companies, had committed £144m to the clubs (with £114m already paid), and the total cost to the football clubs was estimated at £455m. But the launch of a National Lottery, in November 1994, dramatically reduced the Trust's spot-the-ball income.

Stadium modernisation was a great opportunity for the building industry (and profiteers inside and outside football). In the early 1990s, football was as much about Alfred McAlpine, Taylor Woodrow and Norwest Holst as it was about Gary McAllister, Chris Woods and Nigel Clough. Football was regularly featured on the business and property pages of national newspapers, as well as in magazines such as *The Economist* and *Construction News*. Newspapers ran lots of speculative stories that simply petered out, including Arsenal's supposed takeover of Wembley Stadium, Wimbledon's emigration to Ireland, and Coventry City's move 15 miles east for a possible ground-share with Leicester City.

Between 1988 and 2007, twenty-four of 102 League clubs moved grounds, mainly as a result of the Taylor Inquiry. Key factors were

"Homely Footba' Ground" Clydebank, 1989

LAGER
DIREC
PLAYERS.
THE FOOTBALL TRUST
This facility has been grant-aided by the Football Trust.
5
6

"Dire Expectations" Crewe Alexandra, 1990

the financial value of the current stadium's land (especially if it was centrally located in an expanding town or city), the opportunities for developing a cheaper site elsewhere, and the chances of getting planning permission for that alternative site. Some clubs decided to stay, raising development money by selling adjoining land for housing (e.g. Brentford), or a supermarket (e.g. Crystal Palace). Blackburn Rovers planned a £12 million redevelopment of three sides of their existing ground but it meant buying several terrace-houses on Nuttall Street and mills at either end of the ground. Other successful clubs wanted to move in order to raise their capacity. In 1997, Sunderland moved from the long-neglected Roker Park (capacity 22,700) to a new stadium (capacity 41,600). Stuart Roy Clarke photographed them all in flux and even held a show at the Royal Institue of British Architects.

Moving grounds was a great opportunity to rethink the whole strategy of stadium design. It raised the question of business partnerships and more effective ways of using outdoor and indoor space. Clubs looked to share new stadiums with other sports clubs, and multi-purpose ideas included golf driving ranges, five-a-side pitches, bowling alleys, conference centres, health spas, squash courts, offices, hotels and multiplex cinemas. It was also a chance to think about facilities for disabled spectators.

The symbolic meaning of football grounds is never more poignant than just before a club moves to a different stadium. After the last match at the old stadium fans hang around, sifting through their memory banks as if they were card-index-files, feeling the tears well up, perhaps even remembering a friend whose ashes had been scattered on the pitch. When Brasenose College evicted Oxford City from the White House Ground in 1988, former City goalkeeper Alf Jefferies made a special journey to the ground, stood in both goal-mouths and reminisced about all the wonderful time he had there over forty years ago.

A stadium closure usually heralded a memorabilia sale. At Leicester City, fans could buy giant polystyrene figures of ex–manager, Martin O'Neill, and former players. At Millwall the ground was thrown open to the public and bids were taken for eleven sets of gates, thirty-seven turnstiles, fifty-three stadium signs, pieces of carpet, a selection of club crests and a few wooden programme-selling booths. Patches of turf and plastic seats were available, but most of the Millwall seating was sold to Peterborough United. On the day of the sale, many fans just stood and stared at the site. Many took photographs.

Millwall's new stadium, the New Den, took only fifty-seven weeks to build. It cost over £15m, and the money came from the Football Trust (£2.6m), Lewisham Council (£2.6m), the sale of the old ground for housing (£5m), the stadium's new management company (£1m), the FA (£250,000) and an underwritten rights issue (£4m). The arena was also designed as a concert venue. At Huddersfield Town's new home, the McAlpine Stadium, two REM concerts brought money into the whole town.

Most new stadiums met with complaints about parking and traffic snarl-ups until they established new match-day routine. A national organisation, the Federation of Stadium Communities (FSC), lobbied on issues of planning applications, parking for residents and general disruption. For instance, higher stands could block the sun from houses or gardens.

Another issue was a new stadium's name. The choices were often sententious (Pride Park in Derby); a traditional local name (Glanford Park in Scunthorpe); the name of a local sponsor (the Britannia Stadium in Stoke).. One trend was to commemorate club stalwarts in some parts of the new ground (e.g. the Tom Finney Stand at Preston). The Madejski Stadium at Reading and the Kassam Stadium at Oxford United were named after club chairmen. And, as Peter Corrigan wryly pointed out in *The Observer*, Bolton's Reebok Stadium was named after one of the club's trainers.

Fans were concerned about production-line stadiums which added to clone-town feelings. Some fans saw them as part of an English trend towards placelessness. The 1996-97 Premier League fans survey found that sixty per cent of spectators rued the lack of atmosphere in all-seated stadiums. The League investigated further and recommended attracting more away-team fans and creating "atmosphere areas" around the ground. Bands were encouraged, and amplifiers put in the stands. There were periodic campaigns for some terracing to be restored, but football's impetus was towards the future.

In the early 1990s, English people were faced with economic recession, negative equity, repossession of houses, war in Iraq, poll tax, unemployment and redundancy. They looked to their football club for some stability. Some rejected the immediacy and nowness of modern popular culture and longed for what they saw as the authenticity of football's past. Or they glorified football's past because the late-1980s had been so awful for modern football. Also, the new generation enjoyed modern facilities and interest was at its highest for years. A new ground was a new ground for anybody who wanted it to be their ground.

Photographer Stuart Roy Clarke had captured the disappearing past at a critical time.

"Both Guided By Their Loyalty" Watford, 1990

Extra Strong Mints
POLO

"The Push For Gwladys" Everton, 1990

"City of Fortunes" Liverpool 1990

"Lone Flag (Life Goes On)" Liverpool, 1990

"A Kind of Avenue of Dreams" Wigan Athletic, 1990

1989 - 1992
The Homes of Football

In these early, formative years, my football mission was all-consuming. It was like sending postcards home to family and friends, saying look how special this is, look how funny that is. And, occasionally, look how sad this is.

"Training Time" Oldham Athletic. 1990

"Tommy Cooper Routine" Oldham Athletic, 1993

"The Memorabilia Seller" Manchester, 1990

"Distinguished Midlands Semi-Final Venue" Aston Villa 1990

"West Ham Crowd" at Villa Park, 1991

"Crystal Palace Fan Laid Low" Wembley Stadium, 1990

"Gazza On England Duty" Wembley Stadium, 1990

"The H'Away The Lads" Newcastle United at Ipswich Town, 1990

"Fully Grown Boys on Patrol" Hull City, 1990

"The Ticket Office" Hull City, 1990

"The Iron-Man Irony All-Yorkshire Derby" Sheffield United v Leeds United, 1990

"Shouting One's Head Off" Millwall, 1991

"The Girl Feels A Part Of It" Sunderland 1991

"Mirror Mirror On The Wall" Burnley, 1991

"Darwen End (Toil)" Blackburn Rovers. 1991

"Splattered Claret Leaves The Table" Burnley, 1991

"Ladies Retiring Room" Bury. 1990

"Square Ball Boardroom" Rochdale, 1990

"A Crack At Bellevue" Doncaster Rovers, 1990

"Shirts On The Line" Reading, 1990

"Simple Terracing" Sunderland 1990

"View From The Terrace" Sunderland 1990

"Uniform For A World Cup Campaign" Stockport County. 1990

"A Pair Of Tickets For The Match" Bologna, Italy World Cup, 1990

"In A Mountain Surround" Coniston, 1990

"Sunset Over Springfield Park" Wigan Athletic, 1990

"Lights On High Over Elland Road" Leeds United. 1991

"Gary Speed, professional footballer" Leeds United 1991

“Welcome To Ewood Park” Blackburn Rovers, 1990

"Fog On The Wear" Sunderland, 1991

"East Corner Fortune" Rangers, 1992

"Long Winter Ahead" Queen Of The South, 1991

"Midsummer Night's Dream" Wycombe Wanderers, 1990

"Reporting From The Ground" Wycombe Wanderers, 1990

"Rain Comes Down" Sheffield Wednesday, 1990

"(This Is The Kop) Before Kick-Off" Liverpool, 1992

PLEASE DO NOT THROW MISSILES
DO NOT GO ON THE PITCH
adidas

"The Kop" Liverpool 1992

Candy
LIVERPOOL
MANX RALLY
Daily Express

"All The Lonely People Part Two" Liverpool 1992

DO NOT GO
ON THE
PITCH
adidas
EQUIPMENT
LIVERPOOL

"All The Lonely People Part Eight" Liverpool 1992

LIVERPOOL
LIVERPOOL
LIVERPOOL

1992 - 2011
I am just going outside and may be some time

This was my 'bulking-up' period. An earlier sense of discovery was replaced by a sense of 'this is what I do". I needed to establish my work and returned time after time to the same grounds, as well as new ones, to add to the narrative and authority of the collection I was assembling.

In a move to promote my work, I set up a museum in the Lake District, even manning it when I should have been out there taking pictures. I regret that to some extent but I was earnest and dedicated and still managed to produce some of my best work.

"Set To Return" Blackburn Rovers, 1993

"The Policeman Aside The Open Kop" Sheffield Wednesday, 1992

"Blood Red Road End" Barnsley, 1993

"Yellow Brick Road" Bradford City, 1992

"The Return Fixture in April" Newcastle United v Sunderland, 1993

"Looking Up" Sunderland. 1996

"King For A Day" Newcastle United. 1993

"Gang of Six Fratton Boys Revelling In It" Portsmouth, 1992

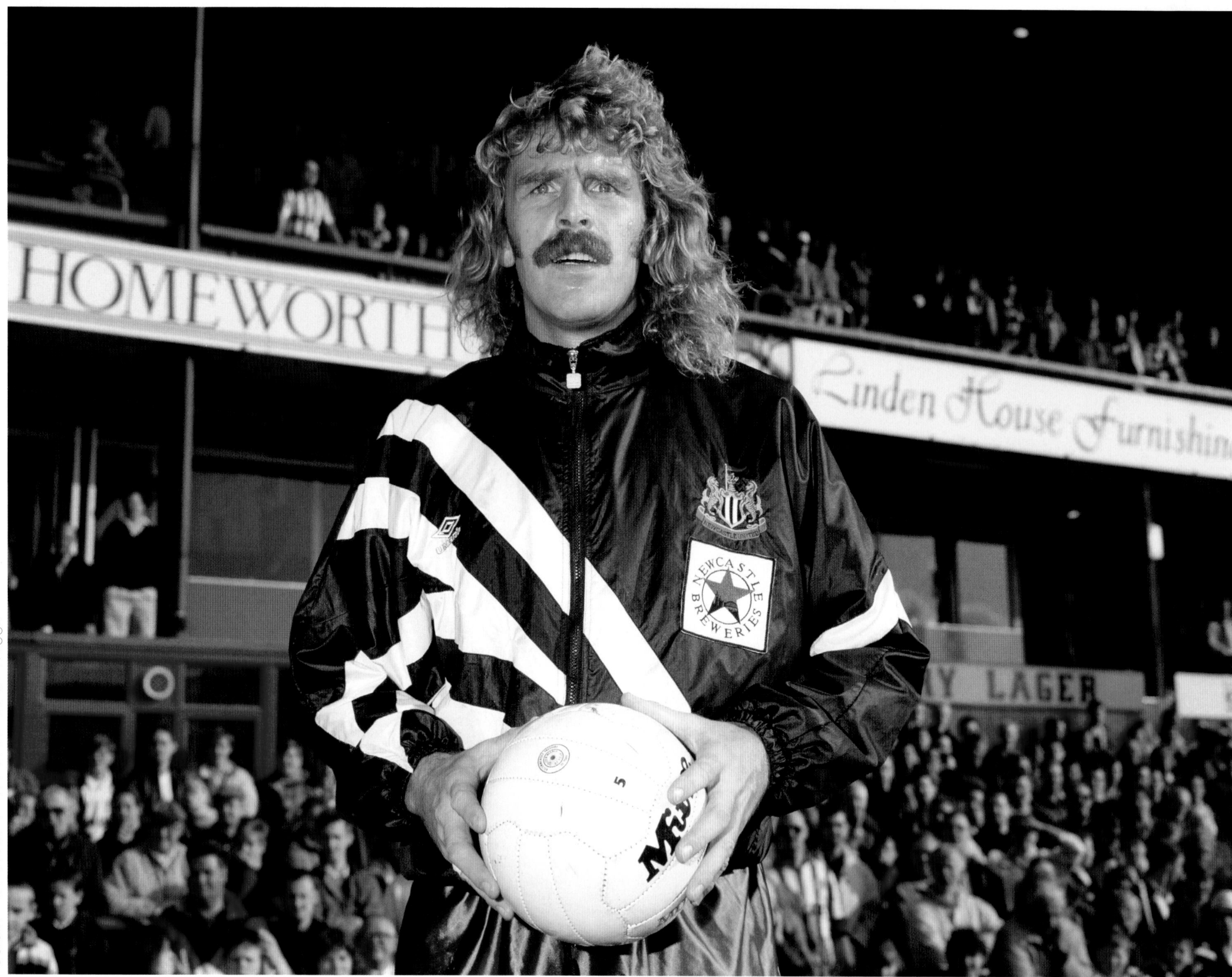

"Goliath" Newcastle United at Sunderland, 1992

"Finding One's Likeness In The Crowd" Sunderland, 1992

"Pitch To Practice On" Craigmark Burntonians. 1996

"Reception Back Hame" Kilmarnock, 1996

"One on One" Greenock Morton v Dundee United. 1996

"Cry For Home" Greenock Morton 1995

"Erstwhile Club Shop" Alloa Athletic, 1996

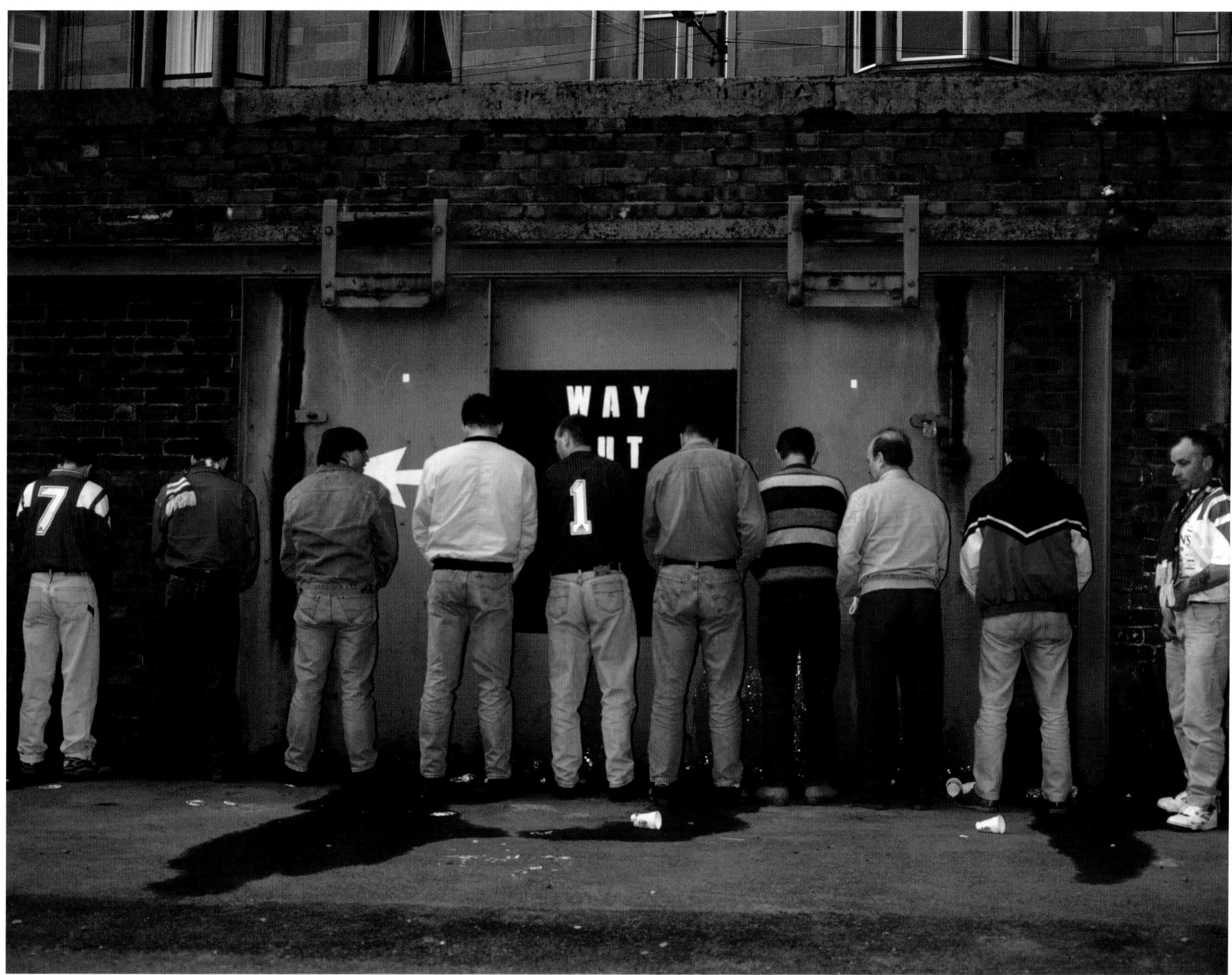

"Allegiance To The Wall" Rangers 1994

"Six Footed Tackle" Celtic v Rangers at Hampden, 1996

"Waiting On The Real Celtic" Celtic. 1994

"Filing The Match Report" Kilmarnock. 1996

"Support From Behind The Goal" East Stirling, 1996

"Celtic Huddle Draws The Terrors" Celtic v Dundee United 1996

LL CLUB 1888
THE BRITISH PRINTING COMPANY LTD
PHOENIX HONDA
TO ADVERTISE
TRAINER
W.A. Wilson
SUPERMART
Semi Chem
UMBRO
CIS INSURANCE
UMBRO
TENNENT'S LAGER
BARR

"Against The Backdrop Of The Big Two" Hibernian v Hearts, 1995

"Sunshine On Leith" Hibernian. 1993

"Penalty Save" England v Scotland at Wembley Stadium. 1996

SCOTLAND 0
ENGLAND 1
PHILIPS
MasterCard
FUJIFILM
VECTRA
JVC
Canon
UMBRO
EUROCARD
SNICKERS
TEKKEN2

"England 2 Scotland 0" M6 Motorway. 1996

"Graffiti In The Shagging Stand" Dalbeattie Star, 1996

"On The Bus" Rangers. 1996

"With A Splash Of Frenchman" Leeds United, 1992

"Big Love On The Neighbourhood" Manchester City, 1993

"Ou Est Cantona?" Manchester United v Swindon Town, 1993

"Days Before The Winter Shutdown" Derby County, 1992

"Somewhere In North Derbyshire Two Lads" 1998

"Ebb & Flow" Grimsby Town v Watford, 1993

"Through Thick & Thin" Swansea City, 1994

"Chelsea's Cheeky Chip" Liverpool 1994

"Going Down At Roker" Sunderland v Newcastle United 1992

"Green & Pleasant Landing" Ambleside United. 1997

"Leeds Road At Twilight" Huddersfield Town, 1993

"Wednesday Getting the Better of United Again" Sheffield Wednesday v Manchester United, 1994

EXIT FORWARD
ON TO PITCH
Wilkin Alarms Ltd
Alexan for Canon
ELECTRICS LTD
LASER
sellec
PUMA
WESTFIELD HEALTH ENCLOSURE
CARLING
SEGA
UNIT TRUSTS
NORTHERN ROCK
Ladbrokes
SANDERSON ELECTRONICS
Lucozade
SILVERWARE
THREE STAR
CRYSTAL PEAKS
Freemans
CABLES LTD
483539

"Last Match Seen From The Corner" Middlesbrough v Luton Town. 1995

SIGMA COATINGS

"Comes To Life" Manchester City, 2002

"With A Gold Handbag" Manchester City, 2003

"Gissa Snog" Everton, 2001

"Licensed Bar" Leigh RMI. 2005

"The Chairman's Dream of Too-Much On His Plate" Carlisle United, 1993

"The Neon Girls" Tranmere Rovers, 1992

"Mark Weekes Eyes Fixed" Aston Villa. 2006

"Tiara And Tutu Tirade" Wolverhampton Wanderers, 2002

"Shepherd's Bush Telegram" Queens Park Rangers, 2003

"Young Mother Red With Pram" 2005

"Prodigal's Return Front Page" Cork City, 2007

"George Best & Co on The Cregagh Road" Belfast. 2005

"Enjoying Each Other's Company" Linfield v Glentoran, 1994

"Boy Looks Back (Going Home)" Barnsley, 1997

"Goalkeeper's View Of The Crowd" Manchester City at Blackburn Rovers, 2000

3:07
Ladbrokes
Official Bookmaker
Hilden
Weaving Quality into Textiles
Hilden
Weaving Quality into Textiles
OVALWORLD
OVALWORLD
J WEST & SONS
OSWALDTWISTLE
MILL
BROCKHALL VILLAGE
Mercer Print
01254 395512
EIDOS

"Police Prepared For The Riotous Assembly" Newcastle United (v Sunderland), 2008

"Boy Looks On The Local Side" Selsey, 2011

"Over The Fence" Sheffield Wednesday, 2010

"That Carlisle Jump" Carlisle United. 2007

"Bunting For Our Hero England" Blackpool. 2010

"Tear From A Window" Glastonbury, 2010

"The Assembled" Ambleside. June 3rd 2010

"Blood Stained Butcher" Glastonbury, 2010

"Family On The Hill" FC United at Colwyn Bay, 2011

"The Away Support" FC United at Buxton, 2010

2012 - 2013
Not Far From The Madding Crowd

Football is a competitive game. Working almost the entire time from my base in The Lake District, gave me a sense of perspective (mountains, emptiness, naturalness) and it gave me a feeling of I will do this on my own terms, in my own time, with no real need to compete. Except against myself.

Then, perhaps because I was now over fifty, and with the economy worsening, I felt I need to get more in touch with the marketplace … and compete. So I moved home to the Peak District, between Sheffield and Manchester, and started producing work of a more gritty, photojournalistic style.

"To Decorate One's Neck" Leeds United, 2012

"A Loving Arm" Sheffield United 2012

"On The Phone Attraction" Manchester City (v QPR), 2012

"On the Pitch Together" Manchester City v QPR, 2012

"Hands On Head At 1-2" Manchester City v QPR 2012

YE08 OBH

"Hanging Out Old Washing" Leeds United, 2012

"Walk Past The Old Gas Works" Huddersfield Town, 2012

"Everyone Up" Sheffield Wednesday, 2012

"Superman And Family" Huddersfield Town, 2013

"A Panic Attack" Sheffield Wednesday, 2012

"The City Is Ours" Sheffield Wednesday, 2012

"Burnley Going Home" Burnley, 2012

"Boy On A Smashed Bus" Burnley at Blackburn Rovers, 2013

"The Fans Know The Way" Blackburn Rovers v Burnley, 2013

"A Chicken Before The Football" Blackburn Rovers v Burnley, 2013

"Clarets Clutch At A Win With Seconds To Go" Burnley at Blackburn Rovers, 2013

"Ever The Young Lady (Next Door)" Blackburn Rovers, 2013

"Sister Christine In Full Shout" Oldham Athletic (v Liverpool) 2013

"The Drummer Didn't See It" Wigan Athletic, 2013

WIGAN
ATHLETIC

"A Day of Judgement" Barnsley at Huddersfield Town, 2013

"The Rising For Sir Alex & Co" Manchester United 2013

"The Old Times Are Over (New York Beckons)" Rotherham United. 2013

"Tied To The Mast Of Their Ship" Port Vale, 2013

"Celebrating in Each Their Own Way" Port Vale, 2013

"It Comes Down To Two" Port Vale. 2013

"A Reet Good Evening Out" Shildon v Dunston, 2013

"Champion Day Out on The Turf" Cardiff City at Burnley. 2013

"He's Saved Up To Buy The Lot" Hull City, 2013

"He's Invested In A Crate" Hull City. 2013

M

"Each Leading the Other On" Bayern Munich v Borussia Dortmund at Wembley, 2013

Index

Here follow my words about the photographs. I feel I have something to say about *all* these pictures. I hope there is something here for students of photography as well as those who are passionate about football and its romance, history and drama.

SRC

Page 6 "One Way Home" Stockport County 1990 *cat.337*
Had I drunk at all - and gone on to get really drunk, for I am an obsessive person, I might never have got very far with the football project. I was always conscious that a pint of beer could cost me a film in my camera - or my driving licence - or an eye in a turning-out time street fight. 'Drink' had probably denied me knowing my two grandfathers who were really interesting characters - so I in turn denied drink, which is a big part of football culture.

Page 9 "Homely Footba' Ground" Clydebank 1989 *cat.2*
I was sent to Scotland by *20-20* magazine to do a story about Scottish band *Wet Wet Wet* growing up on the outskirts of Glasgow and the River Clyde, in Clydebank and Drumchapel. I was given three instructions: *get the crane where the shipyards used to thrive, get the Singer sewing-machine factory where the mums worked, and get something of the football.* Having got the first two I spent most of the weekend bumping into the football. It was intertwined in all the lives of the people around here - not just Marti Pellow and the boys. Football, like it or not, is a huge part of the lives of so many.

Page 10 "Dire Expectations" Crewe Alexandra 1990 *cat.53*
1956 was a great year for me. I wasn't even born but my Mum and Dad moved into a brand new semi on a hill with a great view and woods and fields behind - a house I can still call home. This continuity has given me a great foundation and security.

I grew up surrounded by football and loved it. I was never the first choice in my Sunday team and spent much of my time as an onlooker. My dad was the football league fixture secretary and later chairman and, in these capacities, took me to all manner of games where I started photographing the action both on and off the field.

But, I told myself, football is not a serious subject. It is back page stuff. I thought I should be concentrating on the Miners' Strike, social injustice, politics, revealing the truths about inequality. I was looking for my subject and looking for a base where I could be a valued photographer. In my desperation, I thought I would try my hand at being a fisherman ... but the boats were grounded during two weeks of storms. Photography to me had a unique capacity to reveal beauty so, with no boats to sail I decided to go and take a look at THE most beautiful place in England, so everyone told me. I had never been to the Lake District but it was about to become my home and play a huge part in everything that I did thereafter.

Having found the Lake District, I wanted to stay. Get to the bottom of that unfathomable beauty. I found a job working in a hotel, only to be faced with a hotel owner, who kept sacking everyone - well all the girls anyway. He just sat there with his new fangled television remote control, flicking channels in between sacking people. I was cleaning out the living-room fire with the vacuum cleaner and generally grovelling around his feet when I saw on the television a news flash about a fire at a football match ... Bradford City. It caught my attention but not the owner's, who cursed and changed channels. Another disaster befell football weeks later, halting the hotel staff table tennis tournament. This was Heysel. It all seemed so unjust.

Four years one and football became even more tragic with **HILLSBOROUGH**. People I knew or had met had been there. People I would never meet had been there.

Football then was to be my subject. It had been there all along, just waiting for me to notice it in its fullest sense and to take it seriously and not just as a glorious distraction.

Though I started *The Homes of Football* in moody monochrome, I soon decided it had to be in glorious colour. This football adventure would be serious... but it would be engaging and personal.

Page 13 "Both Guided By Their Loyalty" Watford 1990 *cat.1*
In March 1990, I turned away from black and white and returned to the club of my youth. My first picture would be on the corner turning towards the Vicarage Road ground, a place of ritual and a rite of passage for me. It so happened a well-known blind fan, Dave, was coming up the road with his guide-dog, wearing the brightly coloured shoes that club chairman Elton John had personally given him. Perfect - the first picture would touch on what the whole project was going to be about: the loyalty inherent in football. The caption was easy!

Page 14 "The Push For Gwladys" Everton 1990 *cat.164*
When I began *The Homes of Football* I did it very much with my own cultural review of the game running alongside the Lord Justice Taylor Report (into

Hillsborough). Street talk, loose talk, newspaper talk had been of fans arriving too late - too close to kick off - the cause of it.

Most of 'the causes' were discounted in time. At the time, and since, I can't help feeling uncomfortable about any sort of crush in or around a football ground.

Page 15 "City of Fortunes" Liverpool 1990 *cat.160*
Much is made of Liverpool people's sense of humour. And that stands for the English as a whole. Within the British Islands, all four nations: the English, Scots, Welsh and Irish have this healthy or rather curious like/dislike of each other. And the four tribes compete a bit and take the rise out of each other, and out of themselves. Laughing at yourself sometimes saves someone else the bother of doing it for you.

Page 17 "Lone Flag (Life Goes On)" Liverpool 1990 *cat.540*
Being lonely, windswept, tired and a bit hungry seemed to bring me closer to some truth I was looking for. Exactly a year on from Hillsborough, I wandered across Stanley Park in Liverpool and came across this - a tree, flags and a couple passing in the distance. It was a kind of communion.

Page 18 "A Kind of Avenue of Dreams" Wigan Athletic 1990 *cat.429*
I was drawn to Wigan, seeing it as an underdog. Fifty years before, George Orwell had written about it. An Old Etonian writing about another England. The idea of Wigan Pier was that it was sort of an end of the World place, at the edge of an abyss. In truth, Wigan Pier was just a place on the canal for loading coal, not a literary landmark. Orwell found the people of Wigan warm and loyal to their town.

Page 20 "Training Time" Oldham Athletic 1990 *cat.24*
There was a fair amount of uproar in the late 1980s and early 1990s when several clubs, including some who went back a long time, installed plastic pitches to combat the wet weather. I suspect their reasons too were to go a bit American, go modern. Luton even hosted American football on their plastic. But the football family hated it.

Page 21 "Tommy Cooper Routine" Oldham Athletic 1993 *cat.1134*
Order was restored at Oldham Athletic and their plastic pitch was rolled up and put away. Boundary Park was returned to grass, almost to the dismay of the then manager Joe Royle, who took a cushion from the directors box to save his fabulous leather shoes getting mucky during a television interview.

page 6

page 9

page 10

page 13

page 14

page 15

page 17

page 18

page 20

page 21

Page 22 "The Memorabilia Seller" Manchester 1990 *cat.20*
One of the biggest occasions in the English football calendar was FA Cup Semi-Final Day, when two matches would decide which of four teams would contest the Final at Wembley. The staging of the matches was a great honour for the chosen ground and, though it varied from year to year, Maine Road Manchester was a repeat venue.

Page 23 "Distinguished Midlands Semi-Final Venue" Aston Villa 1990 *cat.15*
On this day, in April, a time when one often gets a taste of all four seasons of British weather in the course of ninety minutes - and when the light is brilliant for a photographer after the gloom of winter - there was a dramatic mismatch at the legendary semi-final venue. Crystal Palace took on Liverpool who had beaten them 9-0 earlier the same season. Outside the ground, with so much happening inside it (it turned out to be a 4-3 thriller and revenge for Palace) the balloons pirouetted against stand and deep blue sky, making as good a picture as I could possibly have got that day.

Page 24 "West Ham Crowd" at Villa Park 1991 *cat.474*
When confronted with crowds, whom I am given the chance to examine, in my role as accredited photographer, able to patrol the pitch perimeter, I look along the rows and sometimes want no one to see me looking. At other times I want them all to address the camera, just as they would in those old Victorian pictures. I always know as I take any of these crowd shots that time will endow the picture, the faces, the lives once lived - with a melancholy and a slight sadness.

Page 25 "Crystal Palace Fan Laid Low" Wembley Stadium 1990 *cat.417*
There's always this excitement about travelling, about trying to get there. Once there, it's interesting how people handle the big occasions.

Page 26 "Gazza On England Duty" Wembley Stadium 1990 *cat.377*
In the now legendary summer of 1990, Gazza's tears, along with Lineker's boyish charm (and goals) on World Cup duty in Italy, had cemented a nation's love affair with its national football team and indeed the country. And here he was - stood before me at Wembley in the after-match darkness - the man chiefly responsible for this big love-in. In a suit, a long way from Tyneside and at the pinnacle of his career.

Page 27 "The H'Away The Lads" Newcastle United at Ipswich Town 1990 *cat.223*
On the beach at Bournemouth in May 1990, just before that summer's World Cup, I had been surrounded by some not so nice England fans who were, in turn, surrounded by the police, truncheons at the ready. Situations like this prepared me for future encounters but these Geordies, whose team were at the bottom of the Second Division and facing relegation, were as nice as pie. I used my waist-level camera and made them look a bit like heroic characters in an early Soviet poster.

Page 28 "Fully Grown Boys on Patrol" Hull City 1990 *cat.309*
During the Miners' Strike, I, like many of my generation, saw the police as a repressive force. Over the twenty-five years of working on *The Homes of Football*, I have had my faith gradually restored.

Page 29 "The Ticket Office" Hull City 1990 *cat.215*
The English have a thing about sheds. Why build a building fit for the purpose when you can knock something together cheaply with a few bits of wood?

Page 30 "The Iron-Man Irony All-Yorkshire Derby" Sheffield United v Leeds United 1990 *cat.166*
Vinnie Jones, the hard-man, grew up near where I grew up and played for a team we used to play against on the (financially) poorer side of Hemel Hempstead. I am curious how a plodding hard man, seemingly a Sunday League bruiser, can compete with an increasingly athletic bunch of teammates and adversaries. I head to Sheffield to watch him amongst equals.

Page 31 "Shouting One's Head Off" Millwall 1991 *cat.510*
'The bravest animal in the land', starts some children's tale. In football-speak the word "Millwall!" when uttered has you close the curtains and slam the book shut. I have the chance to go there to The Den and even move amongst or above the infamous crowd. My mission is surely to paint them black. But I add flashes of white...

Page 32 "The Girl Feels A Part Of It" Sunderland 1991 *cat.551*
I am back in the North East, the foundry of football. As a student, a decade before, I often stayed there with a friend's sister. Though from a posh school, Margaret had been sent here to experience a different kind of finishing school by her mum, who was from these parts and steeped in life's hard lessons. The student-nurses house backed on to Roker Park, home of Sunderland FC. One January night, I was in the bathroom and had an almost religious experience as light from Roker Park flooded through the window. A R-O-A-R shook the glass and the force almost pinned me against the wall. On that rainy day in April, I experienced the essence of what I had been romanticising about all those years.

Page 33 "Mirror Mirror On The Wall" Burnley 1991 *cat.428*
In 1989, when I started *The Homes of Football*, the whole map of the UK on the floor before me, and looked for the heart of football. I kept coming up with Burnley. This is from someone who had grown up in the south. Burnley was in my Soccer Stars album. It was one of the founding clubs of the Football League and had been Champions of all England around the time I was born. It was a town of some 80,000 people and the club, with its famous claret strip, was one of the founding members of the Football League and they had been Champions of England in 1959-60. At the time, Burnley were in Division 4 but the photograph suggested to me, *'you have been the fairest in the land, your mirror is cracked but I, and many others see something extra fair in you'.*

Page 34 "Darwen End (Toil)" Blackburn Rovers 1991 *cat.352*
The proud Chairman stood there in the Blackburn Rovers oak-panelled boardroom telling the story of how football was born out of a spring in a hill near Darwen, which travelled into Blackburn, before going on to populate all parts of the World. I think he really believed this story. He and others who ran football clubs back in the early 1990s had made a few bob either running or owning some industry or other, usually within sight of the club they'd supported in their youth.

Page 35 "Splattered Claret Leaves The Table" Burnley 1991 *cat.438*
Back in the beginning, when I arrived at a club, one of my first questions was to ask which players had been born locally. I imagined them living within sight of the ground, walking to the match, carrying polished boots, amongst their supporters, the people they had grown up with.

Page 36 "Ladies Retiring Room" Bury 1990 *cat.171*
Ladies' Retiring Room. Where did this come from? A reminder of distant days when the sight of a woman might induce panic amongst the assembled men? At least they provided a 'retiring room', not all clubs did.

Page 37 "Square Ball Boardroom" Rochdale 1990 *cat.173*
I was made very welcome in the boardroom, where the men were jovial and where the pretty waitresses came in and out with cakes and desserts and poured the men drinks.

Page 38 "A Crack At Bellevue" Doncaster Rovers 1990 *cat.218*
One of my favourite photographs. Doncaster was, at the time, the worst team in the four divisions and playing at one of the worst grounds. It was a disaster of a football club and, somewhere inside, through that heavenly crack in the gates, Billy Bremner was smoking his guts out in his manager's office, telephone in hand trying to tie up some loan signing.

Page 39 "Shirts On The Line" Reading 1990 *cat.205*
Climbing up the floodlight pylon on a non-match day, having a good poke around an old ground, I looked upon an old guy pinning a notice on a ground notice board (top left). I looked too at the line of houses bang up against Elm Park ground, and observed that one of the local ladies washed the club kit.

Page 40 "Simple Terracing" Sunderland 1990 *cat.107*
Sunderland supporters, of all ages, staring with anticipation at the green rectangle, expecting some great play.

Page 41 "View From The Terrace" Sunderland 1990 *cat.108*
Turning the other way, away from the heavenly green, I looked upon the city of Sunderland and its high rise accommodation as well as cranes which spoke of industry present or past. The lad rode round and around the block on his bicycle. I felt he was imagining what it was like along these very streets and back alleys back in 1966 when Sunderland had staged the World Cup here and everyone would have walked (or cycled) these cobbles to the ground in a throng of humanity. The tent in the back garden looks a little out of place, sad even.

Page 42 "Uniform For A World Cup Campaign" Stockport County 1990 *cat.96*
The summer of 1990 and I was realising the effect the national team and the World Cup could have on a nation. Like many I had been a bit dismissive of England preferring to concentrate on the fortunes of club football and, in particular, my Watford FC. Outside Stockport County's ground, I noticed this mother and son walking down the street. Apparently, all the children were being allowed to go to school in England football kits.

Years later, Bobby Robson, England's manager at the World Cup, asked me about the significance of the photograph. He was amazed by how the nation had reacted while his team were holed up in hotels waiting for their next match.

Page 43 "A Pair Of Tickets For The Match" Bologna, Italy World Cup 1990 *cat.77*
In Italy, I had witnessed first-hand England fans abroad. Not always a pretty sight with their ill-fitting clothes, sunburn and mosquito bites. The police treated them like hooligans, prodding them in the chest with their batons and making them drop their shorts. Their fellow Italian fans, in their stylish clothes, were just waved through.

Page 44 "In A Mountain Surround" Coniston 1990 *cat.43*
Back home, I slept outside in the old stand at Coniston. A communion. I was sick of everyone harping on about the amazing Italian grounds they had seen flashed across their television screens – even though I had seen them close up and they were indeed impressive. These World Cup stadiums were mostly new or rebuilt at great cost. I understood the temptation to start condemning our own grounds in Great Britain as inferior, but I felt annoyed that some of our grounds' history and unique charms were being overlooked - even routinely demolished. What better ground than Shepherdsbridge for instance, where one had to cross a brook via a rickety old bridge and a welcoming sign to get to the football field? Bordered by a bank that could easily hold 100,000 people. Where one could sleep the night in that old stand.

Page 45 "Sunset Over Springfield Park" Wigan Athletic 1990 *cat.201*
This picture really sold *The Homes of Football* to a lot of people when they bumped into it. It had a sunset (which everyone is drawn to) and it spoke of the football spectacle in a gentle way, contrasting with my (verbal) story of the industrial struggle and Orwell, Wigan Pier and all. The picture seemed and seems even now nostalgic and smacks very much of the green, green grass of home ideal.

Page 46 "Lights On High Over Elland Road" Leeds United 1991 *cat.737*
I realised that football was inching its way towards something more glamorous than it had in the 1980s. Leeds had the tallest diamond-shaped floodlights in the country. I photographed them as if they should be on a chocolate box.

Page 47 "Gary Speed, professional footballer" Leeds United 1991 *cat.609*
Gary pulled himself away from his bosom pal and twin midfielder, David Batty, just for this moment, so that I could get his portrait.

Page 48 "Welcome To Ewood Park" Blackburn Rovers 1990 *cat.52*
In my photographs, I play on the fact that *the times they are a changing* and that prices, signs, will soon be out of date and the cause for some bemusement or melancholy in a year or so. Blackburn Rovers and their Ewood Park seemed to make a living out of living in the past, like something out of a Hovis advert. I have always loved the place. You kind of know what you are going to get.

Page 49 "Fog On The Wear" Sunderland 1991 *cat.719*
I love the autumn light in England when everything is bathed in a warm, orange light.

Page 50 "East Corner Fortune" Rangers 1992 *cat.980*
As the English grounds began to change in the first couple of years after Hillsborough and the Taylor Report, I found myself ever more drawn to Scotland, where change would be slower and one could step back in time. Glasgow Rangers were the exception, having already made the great leap forward with a fantastic state of the art ground.

Page 51 "Long Winter Ahead" Queen Of The South 1991 *cat.717*
In Scotland, many of the clubs (unlike in England) have names that bear no relation (except in the hearts of those who named them) to where the club is from. Who in England knows the whereabouts of Queen of The South (Dumfries, resting-place of Robert Burns) and that they are nicknamed The Doonhamers? They are nicknamed *Doonhamers* because when the good people of the area used to go up to big tough Glasgow seeking work and were asked where they came from, they would answer *from doon hame* (down home).

Back in 1992, on my first North Country tour, I predicted tough times ahead for the impoverished clubs of Scotland, bereft of the support they used to enjoy. Twenty-one years later, I am predicting much the same again.

Page 52 "Midsummer Night's Dream" Wycombe Wanderers 1990 *cat.254*
So popular was the match at the new ground, some were driven to the woods and hills to get a vantage point.

Page 53 "Reporting From The Ground" Wycombe Wanderers 1990 *cat.247*
A few days before the previous picture (you can see the woods and the felled tree in the background) *this* had been the scene. What happened was that just two hours before the game was due to go ahead, snow swept across the Chiltern Hills and south-east England and John Motson, not well-known as yet for his sheepskin coat, was doing a live broadcast (fairly rare in those pre-Sky days) to the watching world on BBC1.

The television piece and coat are a sensation. I got the still photo having prised open an exit gate. The match was postponed but went ahead on a balmy evening a few days later, hence the previous picture.

Page 55 "Rain Comes Down" Sheffield Wednesday 1990 *cat.312*
If there's a place and a photo that stops me in my tracks, it is this one. Boxing Day and two years on from Hillsborough, the terraced cage where the manslaughter occurred is still unused. The rain lashes down and is bouncing off the infamous Leppings Lane End. Elsewhere, as I shiver and I shudder, all over the country, families are waiting for loved ones who have gone to watch a match and who have slipped out of the festivities for a while.

Page 57 "This Is The Kop Before Kick-Off" Liverpool 1992 *cat.789*
Back in Liverpool. At home at Anfield, the crowd is awaiting their kick-off.

Page 59 "The Kop" Liverpool 1992 *cat.791*
The Scousers take no prisoners, without first tickling their sense of humour, wherever they can find it.

Page 61 "All The Lonely People Part Two" Liverpool 1992 *cat.794*
As I stand before this great tribe with the privilege of being a photographer, I realise the enormity and significance of the Kop coming together.

Page 63 "All The Lonely People Part Eight" Liverpool 1992 *cat.801*
A policeman passes by.

Page 66 "Set To Return" Blackburn Rovers 1993 *cat.1176*
In Blackburn they have to make way for some new stands, for local enthusiast, fan and owner of a steel empire - Jack Walker - is going to help propel his club back into the top flight of English football.

Page 67 "The Policeman Aside The Open Kop" Sheffield Wednesday 1992 *cat.1050*
The police were heroic in pulling people from the stand at Valley Parade.

Page 68 "Blood Red Road End" Barnsley 1993 *cat.1174*
Barnsley try to keep up with the neighbours with various grant-aided ground improvements. And what they can't rebuild, or don't want to, they chuck a bucket of blood red paint over, with some new shards of glass thrown in.

Page 69 "Yellow Brick Road" Bradford City 1992 *cat.1000*
Walking around the ground which had experienced an horrific fire seven years before, but had been largely rebuilt, I am taken by the sight of the yellow steps installed after the Taylor Report to help people at all grounds find a way to safety (during the Valley Parade fire many people were lost in the smoke). The steps appear magical to my camera as if all of football could be led to a better place.

Page 70 "The Return Fixture in April" Newcastle United v Sunderland 1993 *cat.1147*
Both teams were at this time in the second tier of English football, missing out on being members of the first Premier League clutch of teams. But in building expensive new stands (Newcastle) and a whole new stadium (Sunderland), the marketing plan as well as the fan expectation is for Premiership football - and not just for sliding about in the mire.

Page 71 "Looking Up" Sunderland 1996 *cat.2777*
Football at the Roker Park ground is coming to an end in 1996 and the club and supporters are about to move house. I waited for the fans to spot the spaceship descending from the heavens - their new transport - before making my final portrait of fandom and innocence at the mighty and modest Roker.

Page 72 "King For A Day" Newcastle United 1993 *cat.1162*
Andy Cole is dashing about St James Park - as well as away grounds - scoring at will in a glorious season. Now finished. Now won. On a lap of honour, I ask him to stand still with the League trophy. Behind me is a bank of 6,000 supporters.

Page 73 "Gang of Six Fratton Boys Revelling In It" Portsmouth 1992 *cat.854*
Portsmouth has for centuries been the centre of England's great naval achievements and this is reflected in the dual allegiance these fans show for club and city.

Page 74 "Goliath" Newcastle United at Sunderland 1992 *cat.1034*
I like the humour in this pair of pictures where I turn the one way then the other, to see what the player (Goliath) is looking at. The fierce rivalry of the two North East clubs is invariably laced with dark humour.

Page 75 "Finding One's Likeness In The Crowd" Sunderland 1992 *cat.1035*

Page 76 "Pitch To Practice On" Craigmark Burntonians 1996 *cat.2299*
Nowhere in Great Britain is tougher on the body and mind than the agricultural-rich fields of Ayrshire. For here men not only follow the plough, but are involved in mining, steel, aviation and shipbuilding. From these parts came that great manager, Bill Shankly, and his many footballing brothers.

Page 77 "Reception Back Hame" Kilmarnock (v Falkirk) 1996 *cat.3135*
When two clubs which were neither Celtic nor Rangers get to compete for the Scottish Cup Final in 1996, whole communities breakfast on the occasion and my heart for one is filled with that sense of belonging and connectivity rarely bettered outside of the football experience.

Page 78 "One on One" Greenock Morton v Dundee United 1996 *cat.2373*
Despite my romanticising the Scottish game for all its values of humour and warmth and relatively consistently good attendances, I am forever worried the game will go away from the land that helped shape the game for the world. In this photo, I crop out with my camera all the other players so it looks like the game is reduced to a player a side.

Page 79 "Cry For Home" Greenock Morton 1995 *cat.1958*
Few clubs win anything and it is rare day like this that fans can savour. Greenock Morton had toppled the league leaders but there is a sting in the tail for this young supporter as he waits with red raw arms for his bus to arrive. In tears, he realises that is not going to come. The old guy further back, has seen and experienced this sort of thing before, and is actually on the way to see his new girlfriend! (I learnt this from his grandson who contacted me to tell me his story). The new romantic will get a lift from someone amongst the many who have known him down through the years. The younger boy is still in his apprenticeship.

Page 80 "Erstwhile Club Shop" Alloa Athletic 1996 *cat.2278*
I put in the word *erstwhile* to get me out of being sued by a proud member of Alloa Athletic who might object at the seeming running down and mickey taking of his club.

And he did (object). But the truth is the shop was in this state whilst still in use.

Page 81 "Allegiance To The Wall" Rangers 1994 *cat.1410*
Throughout the 1990's, I worked on a retainer for the Football Trust and then the Football Foundation. Their remit was to return some of the government's tax scoop on the football pools to the game by way of grant-aided projects. I got to photograph them all. The Trust particularly liked the way that I was showing human use of the facilities on which millions of pounds of public money was being spent.

But you can lead a horse to water. These (Rangers) fans are at Hampden, the Wembley of Scotland, replete with very expensively refurbished toilets just yards away, but doing what they have always done.

Page 82 "Six Footed Tackle" Celtic v Rangers at Hampden 1996 *cat.2219*
The matches between Glasgow Rangers and Glasgow Celtic, from either end of the city, with religious affiliations, are legendary. Gazza, the English hero, joins the fray but is set upon by three hoops. These games can be as good as it gets in British football.

Page 83 "Waiting On The Real Celtic" Celtic 1994 *cat.1392*
Before Celtic re-emerge as a modern world class club, they suffer some pain. In 1994, the fans stay away in an attempt to remove the board accused of avoidably dragging the club to bankruptcy. I witness many of the fans returning, with some scepticism and with some blind faith, for a match with Motherwell.

Page 84 "Filing The Match Report" Kilmarnock v Celtic 1996 *cat.2135*
A member of the press telephoning through his match report at the end of the match. I am a bit of an outside, not a member of their ranks, a bit of a maverick with my own tale to tell.

Page 85 "Support From Behind The Goal" East Stirling 1996 *cat.2929*
Most press photographers attending matches are bound to deadlines. I carved out a brief for myself where I would take photographs where my instincts led me, taking as long as it would take, often revealing pictures weeks or months after they were taken.

Page 86-87 "Celtic Huddle Draws The Terrors" Celtic v Dundee united 1996 *cat.2168*
On this occasion I climb up on to the roof of Celtic Park and, lying amongst the floodlights fixed to the main stand, gaze down on all beneath me.

Page 88 "Against The Backdrop Of The Big Two" Hibernian v Hearts 1995 *cat.1997*
Without supporting any one club whilst doing *The Homes of Football* - indeed coming to love them ALL - I side more often than not with the underdog. It's slightly strange that the capital of Scotland has two club sides that both play second fiddle to the two bigger clubs of the second city Glasgow.

Page 89 "Sunshine On Leith" Hibernian 1993 *cat.1214*
I took this title from the song by The Proclaimers - who may well be down there, beneath me, in the crowd on this glorious day.

Page 90-91 "Penalty Save" England v Scotland at Wembley Stadium 1996 *cat.2540*
Being in the right place at the right time is part of the photographer's brief, even if one has a rolling stone agenda. The right place was always going to be Euro1996 held in England at a time of monumental growth in affection for the national game. And then they go and get drawn against age-old rivals Scotland. Then there is a penalty called. I am level with the action as the (Scottish) crowd behind the goal breathe in so desperately that they unwittingly suck the well-struck ball off course and into England goalkeeper Seaman's grasp. Gazza, who plays in Scotland at this time, is about to collect this gifted ball on the halfway line and take it all the way to the Scots' net at the other end. You can't be in the right place all the time!

Page 92 "England 2 Scotland 0" M6 Motorway during Euro 1996 *cat.2550*
Returning home, as I cross the England/Scotland border, I get some extra action as a lorry announces the score to all who follow.

Page 93 "Graffiti In The Shagging Stand" Dalbeattie Star 1996 *cat.2297*
I like to boast that attending a miniscule game in rural Scotland will surely return me as good and as popular a picture as I have taken anywhere in Scotland, or beyond. I like to think that every time I go anywhere, however small, with the camera there is the possibility of a big catch. Robbie Williams, a well-known English singer and fan of football, summons me to his show at Barrowlands to show him my wares during rehearsal (he flexing his muscles parading the length of the stage, looking down at the pictures laid out on the floor). This picture now hangs in his bathroom.

Page 94 "On The Bus" Rangers 1996 *cat.2231*
I shot this photograph of Rangers waving goodbye on instinct. Sixteen years later, it took on an extra significance when Rangers were declared bankrupt and demoted to the Scottish 4th Division.

Page 95 "With A Splash Of Frenchman" Leeds United 1992 *cat.951*
Eric Cantona joins the triumphant Leeds United team managed by Yorkshireman Howard Wilkinson and together they all become the English champions, against all odds.

Cantona moves on to Manchester United where he and club usurp this other United of their title. Leeds finish 17th in 1993 and are nearly relegated.

Page 96 "Big Love On The Neighbourhood" Manchester City 1993 *cat.1226*
Coronation Street with the football for good measure.

Page 97 "Ou Est Cantona?" Manchester United v Swindon Town 1993 *cat.1257*
Cantona will later become infamous for jumping into the crowd at Crystal Palace. Here, against Swindon, he is over the barricades and at one with his United fans of Old Trafford. Said Cantona of English grounds, comparing them to anywhere else: *You are closer to the public. It is warmer. There is room for love.*

Page 98 "Days Before The Winter Shutdown" Derby County 1992 *cat.779*
When I took this picture, there was much talk of English football having a winter break: to refresh players, help pitches recover, and to move some of the season towards the summer. But this has not happened in the twenty and more years since.

Page 99 "Somewhere In North Derbyshire Two Lads" 1998 *cat.4194*
Much of the charm and wonder of British football is that there are so many clubs representing the neighbourhoods in which they organically grew up.

Page 100 "Ebb & Flow" Grimsby Town v Watford 1993 *cat.1238*
Grimsby's ground, Blundell Park, is situated next to the North Sea, at the mouth of the Humber estuary where the rivers Ouse and Trent empty into it.

Page 101 "Through Thick & Thin" Swansea City 1994 *cat.1429*
The two brothers keep the flag flying for their team who are playing Fulham in League Division Three. In the top right hand corner, some fans make their way to the match from the pub (whilst others loiter) and, in the ground, a man has a corner all to himself, his own special place. The Vetch Field is located cheek by jowl with the neighbourhood. A ground now gone.

Page 102 "Chelsea's Cheeky Chip" Liverpool 1994 *cat.1390*
After more than a decade in the wilderness, Chelsea begin to impress in the top flight of English football. They take on the (then) most successful club ever, before the mighty Kop.

Page 103 "Going Down At Roker" Sunderland v Newcastle United 1992 *cat.1039*
Which grounds are the best and which derby occasions are the best are the sort of things much talked about and much prized. The encounter of the North East's foremost rivals, even when competing in the second tier, is a hard derby to beat. I climb to the highest position, even above the television cameramen with their flasks, to get a view which includes a panorama of the North Sea. A fan, for his part, has climbed the floodlight pylon.

Page 104 "Green & Pleasant Landing" Ambleside United 1997 *cat.3244*
Living in the Lake District for the first twenty-four years whilst putting together *The Homes of Football*, I could not ignore with my camera-eye the grounds and games and clubs in my own neck of the woods. Ambleside United, for decades an also-ran in the Westmorland League, go on to rise above the usual list of title contenders: Kendal, Appleby, Coniston, Keswick and Penrith, to become repeat champions and dominate so thoroughly that they simply have to leave the league they had been in for more than 100 years.

Page 105 "Leeds Road At Twilight" Huddersfield Town 1993 *cat.1096*
Here, at Leeds Road, the Terriers had under Herbert Chapman become champions of all England for the third successive season in 1926. Despite being so good, they had nowhere else to go, the Football League was all. Just a few years before, they might have gone up the road to merge with Leeds United, but a public outcry ensued.

Today, Huddersfield Town host Southend United in Round 4 of the FA Cup, January 23rd 1993. Attendance 7,961. This is to be Huddersfield's next to last season at their famous ground, before moving a few hundred metres to the McAlpine Stadium and a whole new history.

Page 106 -107 "Wednesday Getting the Better of United Again" Sheffield Wednesday v Manchester United 1994 *cat.1694*
Football has a new time - 4 p.m. on Sundays - to suit live television coverage (on Sky). Five years have passed since the away end (left) took the lives of ninety-six Liverpool fans. Sheffield Wednesday, and Hillsborough, have a chance to celebrate - they invariably combine to subdue the mighty Reds of Manchester.

Page 108 – 109 "Last Match Seen From The Corner" Middlesbrough v Luton Town 1995 *cat.1773*
Before the last kick-off here at Ayresome Park, past heroes waltz and hobble around the perimeter, milking the applause of a packed house. The name of the new ground is announced (The Riverside) and the Kop sings "You'll never walk Alone". It's almost over for the ground that played host in the World Cup 1966.

Page 110 "Comes To Life" Manchester City 2002 *cat.6438*
Coronation Street aside, the Manchester derby boasts the biggest drama.

Page 111 "With A Gold Handbag" Manchester City 2003 *cat.6702*
Maine Road is in its final days. Fans are issued with Pac A Macs as City readies itself for a new level of customer service.

Page 112 "Gissa Snog" 2001 *cat.5514*
The couple meet, stop for a quick-slow embrace in the streets by Goodison Park. Enter different turnstiles. Moyes will replace Walter Smith later in the season and Everton will finish 15th.

Page 113 "Licensed Bar" Leigh RMI 2005 *cat.7037*
Leigh RMI was one of two football clubs founded at the locomotive works of the Lancashire and Yorkshire Railway; it started at the main works in Horwich (where Bolton now play at the Reebok). The other club was formed at Newton Heath works and later became known as Manchester United.

When this picture was taken, Leigh RMI are at the highest level they have ever played, a year when they also host FC United of Manchester in a friendly for their first ever game. A merger between the clubs is tabled - but relinquished. Leigh is on the demise and trying to grab on to table mats.

Page 114 "The Chairman's Dream of Too-Much On His Plate" Carlisle United 1993 *cat.1306*
He has done so much for the club in such a short spell and he believes it is now his and he can eat it whole. The man who almost bought Manchester United and had a grand plan is denied the bigger feast and has to settle for Carlisle United. Which goes well for a few seasons. Then the club is sold on and he exits stage left and seemingly out of football. A talent lost. The maverick visionary re-emerges in 2012 as an art collector and political commentator, with a sharp eye on football goings-on.

When asked if he minded me using this picture in my book, he answers: "Please do, but please add that I am also a poet and still very much interested in the game".

Page 115 "The Neon Girls" Tranmere Rovers 1992 *cat.0825*
During a boring game between Rovers and Watford I wandered off and discovered these sisters manning the refreshments kiosk. In fact a third sister was at the Cowsheds End of the ground. They are pleased to have their picture taken. They are invited to see their picture in a Museum and turn up with more than a dozen members of their family from the Merseyside area.

Page 116 "Mark Weekes Eyes Fixed" Aston Villa 2006 *cat.7574*
I lean over the hoarding and ask Mark if he minds me having taken his picture and could I use it? He is happy enough. Subsequently it gets put on billboards all over the country as part of an advertising campaign for Sky Sports high definition television. Mark is not a celebrity and is not propelled to stardom by this exposure but it must be quite a thing to have your picture used in such a public way.

Page 117 "Tiara And Tutu Tirade" Wolverhampton Wanderers 2002 *cat.5666*
Having led the pack for the whole season - at one point being way ahead and practically promoted - the Wolves have blown it (yet again). Now, through the play-offs, they have a chance to turn it around. If they don't get the goals then this muscular man will walk home defeated in his tutu and tiara.

Page 118 "Shepherd's Bush Telegram" Queens Park Rangers at Millennium Stadium in Cardiff, 2003 *cat.6743*
The club has been through the mill, whilst their London neighbours have prospered. Much could be said, today is a Cup Final of sorts (the Play-Offs). Sensing a camera, the lady smiles and, by the time her boyfriend finishes jabbering and opens his eyes, the telegram has been sent!

Page 119 "Young Mother Red With Pram" Liverpool 2005 *cat.7123*
I expect to go to Istanbul to see the Champions League Final, but can't. I settle for a drive around Liverpool the following day. Stopping the car, I catch the lady in red in my frame. The *Liverpool Echo* runs the story about a mum and baby having their photograph exhibited in a museum. An added twist, I discover later, is that the baby is dressed in blue. It might have been Liverpool's day but the father is an Everton supporter.

Page 120 "Prodigal's Return Front Page" Cork City 2007 *cat.8425*
Roy's homecoming, as a manager, sets the discussions racing - was he Cork's finest son or a wayward son-of-a-gun? After all, he chose to represent nearby naval town Cobh over his home city.

Page 121 "George Best & Co on The Cregagh Road" Belfast 2005 *cat.7230*
The neighbourhood produced at least five international footballers who they claim as their boys. Derek dancing-shoes Dougan has clearly upset his Protestant peers in a highly-politicised community. George seems to rise above any comparison.

Page 122 "Enjoying Each Other's Company" Linfield v Glentoran 1994 *cat.1427*
When I am photographing football, I'm also interested in the community represented by whatever club. Take the Belfast situation - I like to know a bit about the social setting, the history and the reasons why clubs and grounds and supporters are as they are.

Page 123 "Boy Looks Back (Going Home)" Barnsley 1997 *cat.3137*
It's the first day in the Premiership for Barnsley. No one, in all of Barnsley's history, has seen this before. No one would have planned on them making the Premier League. This is a big deal for a relatively unfashionable town. This changes the way people think of Barnsley and how Barnsley thinks of itself.

Page 124-125 "Goalkeeper's View Of The Crowd" Manchester City at Blackburn Rovers 2000 *cat.4763*
Manchester City fans sing songs such as We're Not Really Here, which on paper might seem a nonsense lyric but makes perfect sense somehow when sung by thousands in unison and you are there to witness it. The City psyche is a strange and wonderful one, taken to the edge of madness by the success of their near neighbours United and their own relative failure.

Almost a year ago to this day, City had a miraculous last gasp win over Gillingham to take them from the third tier of English football to the second. And now, at Blackburn, with their goal peppered by Rovers' chances, they confound again. The City goalkeeper sticks his head through the net to gaze on the *Not Really Here* tribe going out of their minds behind him. In an almost biblical scene, the wounded can suddenly holler, jump, walk.

Page 126 "Police Prepared For The Riotous Assembly" Newcastle United v Sunderland 2008 *cat.8548*
The police will get a lot of stick for this - being so well organised that they insist on taking fans hundreds of metres, if not miles, out of their way to the match and then home thereafter - in order to ensure their safety and the greater peace.

Page 127 "Boy Looks On The Local Side" Selsey 2011 *cat.8797*
The boy feels that this is his club. Relatives are out there on the pitch and all around him are people he knows. He's even allowed to wander freely through the clubhouse.

Page 128-129 "Over The Fence" Sheffield Wednesday 2010 *cat.8662*
Having picnicked, father and daughter jump to it.

Page 130-131 "That Carlisle Jump" Carlisle United 2007 *cat.8364*
The club has known famous last kicks of the game.

Page 132 "Bunting For Our Hero England" Blackpool, 2010 *cat.8694*
Blackpool have just been promoted and now it is England's turn as they prepare for World Cup success, or something, in South Africa.

page 133
page 134
page 135
page 136
page 137
page 140
page 141
page 142
page 144
page 145
page 146-147
page 148-149
page 150
page 151
page 152
page 153
page 154
page 155
page 156
page 157
page 158
page 159

Page 133 "Tear From A Window" Glastonbury, 2010 *cat.8690*
The English just love that phrase *it will surely end in tears.*

Page 134 "The Assembled, Ambleside, June 3rd" 2010 *cat.8664*
Flaming June. Eve of the World Cup. I arrange to photograph everyone outside Churchill's, which, whilst welcoming all, is a deeply patriotic pub. They all want their flags on show - a few of which I have carried to the corners of the earth on the town's behalf. News starts coming through of a gunman on the loose in the west of the county, heading our way over Hardknott Pass. That mad gunman is Derek Bird. Without any irony, the publican is heard to say *'What does he think he is doing – doesn't he know we are trying to organise our flags here'.*

This photograph taken, I feel the need to head to Hardknott Pass and into this madman's path. There is something of the journalist in me after all.

Page 135 "Blood-Stained Butcher" Glastonbury 2010 *cat.8681*
The World Cup collides with the other biggest event - Glastonbury music festival. A third of the 190,000 who will throng to the Somerset farm arrive early, on the Wednesday, to watch England's first match on the big screen. On the Saturday, when England play Germany, two-thirds of the festival goers are watching the must-see game on two big screens. One of the biggest football crowds amassed anywhere in the world.

Page 136 "Family On The Hill" FC United at Colwyn Bay 2011 *cat.8731*
So many people begin to follow FC United as the club works its way up through the tiers below the Football League that, on occasions, their away following is locked out but improvises. Like here in Wales.

Page 137 "The Away Support" FC United at Buxton 2010 *cat.8620*
The dog watches every move. Even moving to behind the goal nets for the second half.

Page 140 "To Decorate One's Neck" Leeds United 2012 *cat.9388*
There is a real sense of permanence every time I take a photograph. People must feel that way about having a tattoo.

Page 141 "A Loving Arm" Sheffield United 2012 *cat.8995*
Love and hate are strange bedfellows.

Page 142 "On The Phone Attraction" Manchester City (v QPR) 2012 *cat.9208*
It's the match versus Queens Park Rangers. May 13th. One to ring your friends about. And taunt your enemies.

Page 144 "On the Pitch Together" Manchester City v QPR 2012 *cat.9211*
For many, not just City fans, history could well be divided into pre-May 13th and post-May 13th. So monumental is the drama, live on screens all over the world.

Page 145 "Hands On Head At 1-2" Manchester City v QPR 2012 *cat.9210*
Given a roving access role by my hosts to capture the day, I realise something very special is unfolding. I have to keep my nerve to see beyond the latest heartache or surprise to get in the right positions to tell the entire story of the day, right to the final kick. I may not get such a chance again.

Come the start of the following season, my pictures, including this one, are displayed large-scale and outdoors for fans returning from their holidays. It is a proud moment for me to see my pictures-on-stilts walked between and touched and looked up to.

Page 146-147 "Hanging Out Old Washing" Leeds United 2012 *cat.9404*
Leeds kick off the new season against relegated Wolves. Both clubs might expect to be in the Premier League as of right. But they aren't.

Page 148-149 "Walk Past The Old Gas Works" Huddersfield Town 2012 *cat.9392*
They'll moan when the dirty old gas works is completely gone.

Page 150 "Everyone Up" Sheffield Wednesday 2012 *cat.8988*
My photographic interest in football is above all about the shared experience.

Page 151 "Superman And Family" Huddersfield Town 2013 *cat.9711*
My interest is in community enveloping personal dreams, wishes and experiences.

Page 152 "A Panic Attack" Sheffield Wednesday 2012 *cat.8988*
I love what Bruce Springsteen (American, never played the game) said and seems to say continuously: *Nobody wins unless we all win.*

Page 153 "The City Is Ours" Sheffield Wednesday 2012 *cat.9175*
Although most clubs never win anything, I still feel throughout the game that we can all be winners.

Page 154 "Burnley Going Home" Burnley 2012 *cat.9528*
As I left the ground, I had a great feeling of communal history, of shared stories told around the fireside in the terraced homes that run down the steep Burnley hillsides.

Page 155 "Boy On A Smashed Bus" Burnley at Blackburn Rovers 2013 *cat.9575*
Someone in a gang had hidden behind the wall and as the convoy of buses passed, hurled all manner of debris they had found in the scrub. The boy looks vulnerable and yet somehow indestructible, almost angelic.

Page 156 "The Fans Know The Way" Blackburn Rovers v Burnley 2013 *cat.9578*
I love the way a crowd can rise up! As long as they don't turn to arms and get things too out of perspective.

Page 157 "A Chicken Before The Football" Blackburn Rovers v Burnley 2013 *cat.9581*
There's trouble at t'mill. Foreign owners! Own a chicken ranch! View this as a franchise.

And today, on top of this, Rovers have to face hungry Burnley who have not won at Ewood for thirty-four years but may be confident that Rovers are distracted.

Page 158 "Clarets Clutch At A Win With Seconds To Go" Burnley at Blackburn Rovers 2013 *cat.9586*
Thirty-four years since Burnley beat Blackburn. Their rivals. Then this matchwinner in front of their bank of travelling fans, with hardly enough time for Rovers to respond.

Page 159 "Ever The Young Lady (Next Door)" Blackburn Rovers 2013 *cat.9582*
I could not imagine her ever getting angry.

Page 160-161 "Sister Christine In Full Shout" Oldham Athletic (v Liverpool) 2013 *cat.9555*
These Latics are treading water or possibly drowning at the bottom of the third tier, and then Liverpool come to town in the FA Cup, on a sleepy Sunday. Something is changed by the Oldham win - an almost religious experience. Life won't seem the same again.

Page 162-163 "The Drummer Didn't See It" Wigan Athletic 2013 *cat.9570*
An unprecedented season for Wigan, now a football town of some standing. They've astounded in the FA Cup and look to be on course to stay in the Premiership. But, in the final hour, they win the cup and are relegated.

Page 164 "A Day of Judgement" Barnsley at Huddersfield Town 2013 *cat.9716*
It has gone to the last match of the season. Either hosts Huddersfield or neighbours Barnsley, or both, or neither, will go down.

Page 165 "The Rising For Sir Alex & Co" Manchester United 2013 *cat.9761*
The last time they won it, it rained and a modest crowd turned out. This time, the rain has cleared and people are on the shoulders of giants, who are on tiptoes.

As the crowd disperses all around me up every road and alley in central Manchester, I am left musing on why so many people would come just to catch a glimpse of a football team, albeit United and Sir Alex saying goodbye. To watch on television is sometimes not enough. You have to *be there.*

Page 166-167 Rotherham United "The Old Times Are Over (New York Beckons)" 2013 *cat.9681*
A man has peaked too early in the day. Or not peaked at all. He may well miss a day like no other up at the new New York (a district of Rotherham) stadium. His side promoted and on their way. Promotion plus a new stadium can drag half the town along with the momentum.

Page 168-169 "Tied To The Mast Of Their Ship" Port Vale 2013 *cat.9657*
Vale were on the bottom and rivals Stoke lunching out with God. But the fans never left the club and now, on this day, versus Northampton, the crew of thousands are about to be promoted.

Page 170 "Celebrating in Each Their Own Way" Port Vale 2013 *cat.9660*
Outpourings of English emotion rarely seen elsewhere in English social life.

Page 171 "It Comes Down To Two" Port Vale 2013 *cat.9662*
What could be better than the shared football experience?

Page 172 "A Reet Good Evening Out" Shildon v Dunston 2013 *cat.9672*
What an adventure, this Northern League, the second oldest in the world, just a tad younger than the Football League.

And for Shildon, who have come close and as close you can get, in every competition in the one season, these are dates to cherish.

Page 173 "Champion Day Out On The Turf" Cardiff City at Burnley 2013 *cat.9642*
1961! The last time the Bluebirds were in the top flight. Turf Moor was a powerhouse. A young Welsh couple hug each other and look forward to the Premiership.

Page 174 "He's Saved Up To Buy The Lot" Hull City 2013 *cat.9728*
Everyone has gone home. The man who bought the club is about to as well. His club has just been promoted to the Premier League. It will be expensive.

Page 175 "He's Invested In A Crate" Hull City 2013 *cat.9729*
Everyone has gone home. Let it sink in. This fan stops by the supermarket. The Premier League will be expensive!

Page 176-177 "Each Leading the Other On" Bayern Munich v Borussia Dortmund at Wembley 2013 *cat.9791*
They have come to Wembley Stadium in England to show off and win the European club crown over their German fellows Borussia Dortmund. Role models both.

Back Cover Page "Swear It's Football" Northampton Town 1990 *cat.148*
The Cobblers share their ground with the County's cricket team. *Is that why the polite notice?* Or the fact that Town went up the four divisions and down the same four divisions in only nine years without ever really recovering.

page 160-161
page 162-163
page 164
page 165
page 166-167
page 168-169
page 170
page 171
page 172
page 173
page 174
page 175
page 176-177
Back Cover

Acknowledgements

My thanks to all the clubs and officials, at all levels, who have readily given me access to their grounds; to John Williams and Andy Ward for allowing me to use their very flattering piece (almost a whole chapter based around me) in their great account of football history *Football Nation* (Bloomsbury Publishing); to John Scott (Giraffe Imaging) for his excellent book design and image preparation; to Digitalab of Newcastle-Tyne for looking after my films; The Chase design agency of Manchester for the green place-names map - and more; to The National Football Museum for championing my collection and keeping it under their glass roof; to Philip French & Martin Hudson & Mark Blackbourne who have guided me. To the Professional Footballers Association and to The Premier League who have consistently backed me.

Thanks to the many football fans who have encouraged me on my journey. And, of course my family. My daughter Ava, now seven, has never been to a match but says she must be in this book. You're in, Ava!

Published by The Bluecoat Press, Liverpool
Printed in China by 1010 Printing Company
Book Design by John Scott/Giraffe Imaging, Newcastle upon Tyne

ISBN 9781908457196